Tip
that hat

Written by Samantha Montgomerie
Illustrated by Jana Costa

How far back do hats go?

For as far back as we can see, we have worn hats.

5,300 years back, this man had a fur hat to keep out the chill!

This thick fur was on the man's hat.

This hat was worn 3,500 years back. We can tell that she was a rich queen. This hat was worn by kings, too.

How to tip a hat

Let's go back 200 years. Men had 'top hats'. Look at how high a top hat was.

Back then, a man had to tip his hat to all the men he met. He did that by tapping the rim of his hat with the tips of his fingers.

But if the man he met was richer than him, he took his hat right off, up high!

Hats for her

This is a 200-year-old bonnet. Back then, bonnets had satin, ribbons, pins and fur on them. Bonnets looked so good.

This hat was pinned high up on a queen's hair. The hat looked as if it was sitting on air.

Posh hats

Hats let you feel good and look posh.

Now, hats can be bigger than ever!

Or not!

Top hats are not worn much now, but a man might have one for a wedding.

Pompoms are fun

A wool hat might have a pompom on top. It might be red or pink or ... all sorts.

Have a go at a pompom

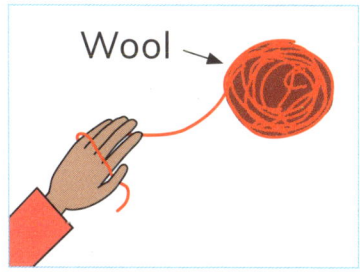
Wool

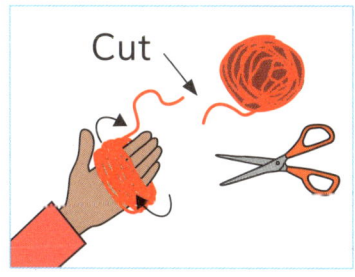
Cut

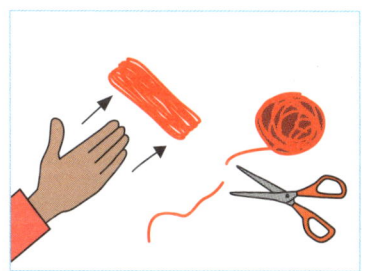

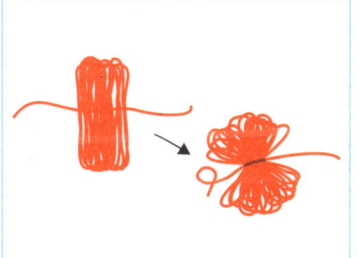

Cut loops

Cut loops

Puff it up!

Bucket hats for the sun and the rain

Do you have a cotton bucket hat? It's a good hat for the summer.
The big rim on a bucket hat will keep the hot sun off your neck.

Have fun in the sun, but keep your hat on!

Back in 1900, fishers had woollen bucket hats to keep the rain off. Yes, bucket hats are that old.

Now, there are cotton bucket hats that have been waxed or oiled to keep the rain off us. And the big rims are good in the rain, too.

Hats for fans

We can pop on a hat and yell,
"Go, Go, Go!"
This lad is a fan of the Reds –
you can tell by his hat.

This cap was worn by batters. Now, it is worn by batters and by fans, too. It might have a mesh panel so that air can get in.

Woollen caps

Woollen caps keep out the chill. This sort of wool cap was worn far back in the 1550s. And it is worn now, too.

In 1571, this queen ordered that all lads and men, older than six years, **had** to pop a wool cap on! How odd!

Hats on!

This woollen cap is worn tipped up a bit.

Cork hats

Have you ever seen a hat with corks hanging off the rim? The corks hit bugs in the air so they cannot get near you. That's good as there are a lot of bugs in the summer.

Cool hats

This cool hat is a 'long horn' hat. Old hair is laid on wood or a horn. Then wool is fixed on the top to keep it all tight.

A record-winning hat

This high hat has the record for high hats right now. It is in America.

The hat is higher than this hoop.

Hats on the job

There are jobs that are hard to do with no hat on.

It can be too hot in the sun with no hat.

Hats keep the chill out, too, so we can keep going.

A hard hat keeps rocks off this man.

This hat has a light on it so she can do her job in the dark.

This hat is worn by cooks. The hat keeps hair out of the food being cooked.

The cool air in the upper part of the hat keeps the cook cooler, too.

It is said that the better the cook is, the bigger her hat will be.

The hat tells us the job that they do.

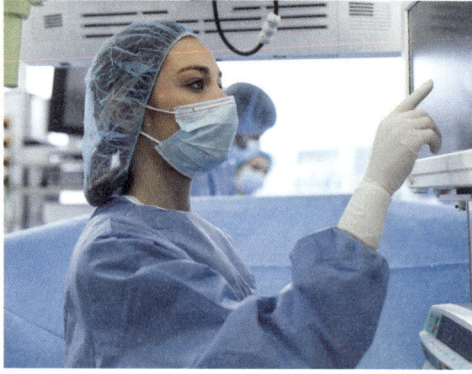

Hat luck

Hats can be bad luck or good luck.

Keep your hat on the boat
Out sailing, if a hat fell off the boat, it was said to be bad luck.

Keep your hat off the bed
A hat on the bed was said to be bad luck, far back. Hair might have had bugs in it. So, if a hat was on the bed, the bugs might have hopped off the hat and onto the bed.

Keep your hat up for good luck

If your hat is down, your luck will get out. But if the hat is up, it will keep your luck in the hat.

Bad luck

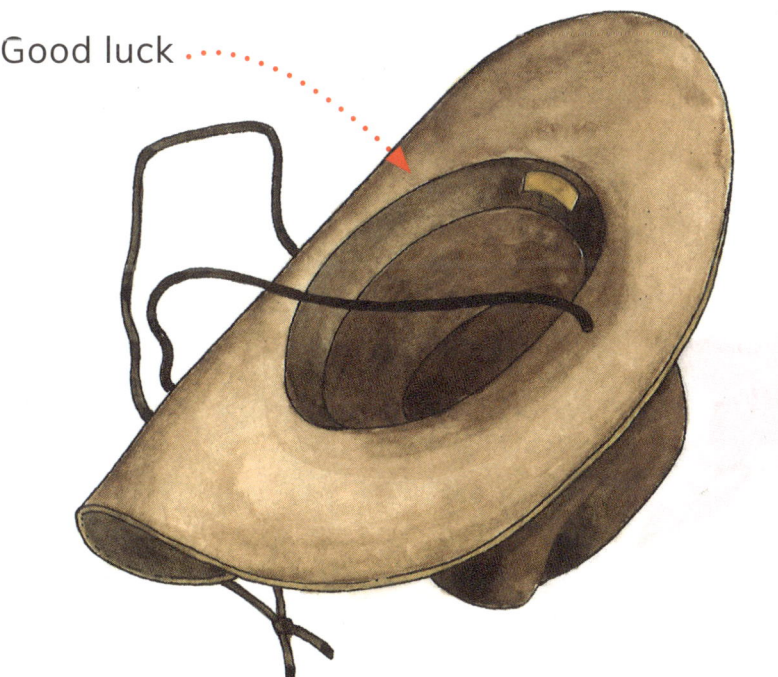

Good luck

Lots and lots of hats

Look at all the hats. Pick one you think looks good.

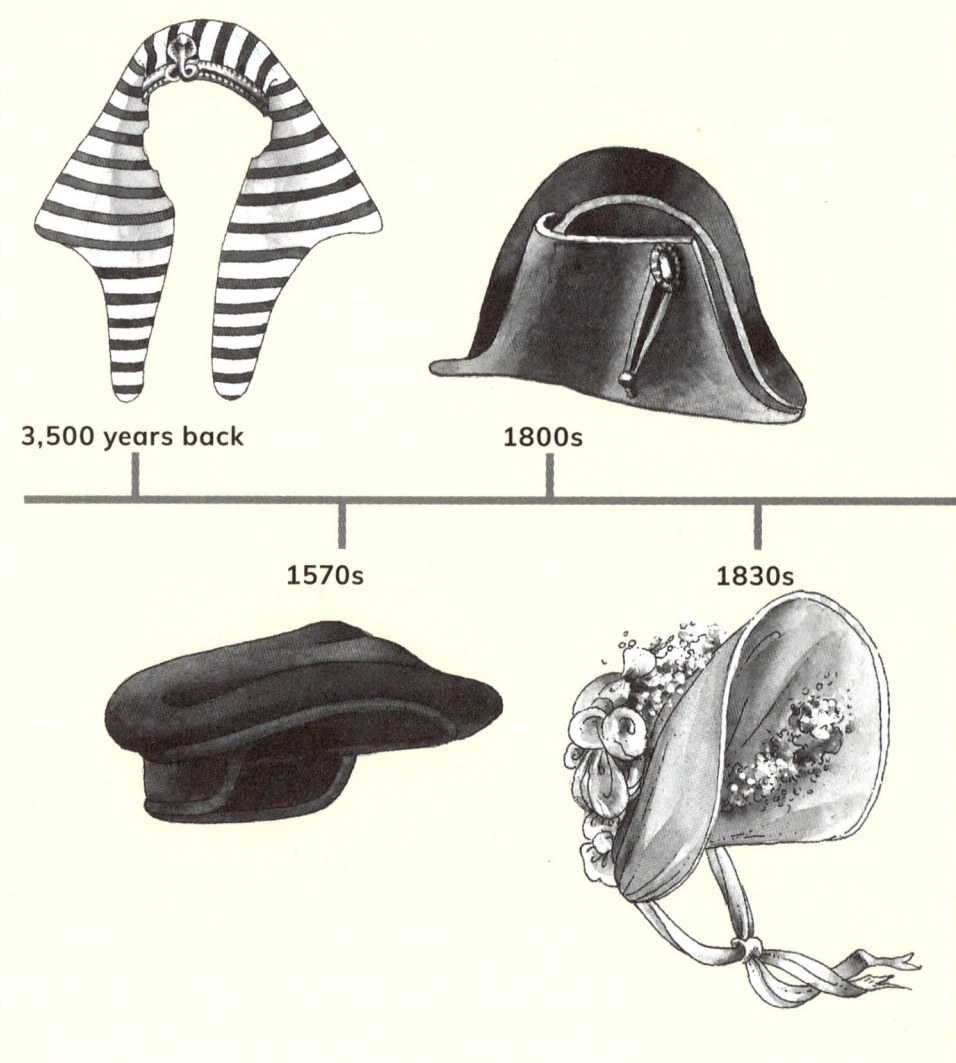

Hats are for all of us

Lots of us have hats.

Hats will be with us for years and years.